The Little Book of Pigs

Vicky Edwards

Pretty pictures by Rob Smith

summersdale

THE LITTLE BOOK OF PIGS

Summersdale Publishers Ltd
46 West Street
Chichester
West Sussex
PO19 1RP
UK

www.summersdale.com

Printed and bound by Proost, Belgium

ISBN 1 84024 391 0

For Duncan

With grateful thanks to David Edwards, Posy and Petrova Fossil and Andy Neal

Contents

A Piggy Prologue

Pigs have had their trotters planted firmly on Earth for donkey's years. One of the oldest mammal species still roaming the planet, they have been around for some forty-five million years, though they were not begun to be domesticated until a mere 8,000 years ago. Then, somewhere around 4,000 BC, the Chinese were instructed to breed pigs by royal decree.

Pigs all come under the heading of 'Suidae', a group that encompasses babirusa, giant forest pigs, wild boars, warthogs and bush pigs. Your regular pink pig is a descendent of the wild boar (*Sus scrofa*) and its posh title is *Sus scrofa domesticus*.

Far from being stupid as is often assumed, pigs are cleverer than most mammals, trumped only by primates and dolphins. Porcine professors certainly rate the brains of boars and many experts claim that pigs are naturally curious and therefore easier to train than dogs. Certainly pigs have been trained to do all sorts of things, including pulling carts, racing, dancing and even playing football. Piglets are very affectionate and older porkers are courageous. Stories of drowning children being rescued by pigs who fancy themselves as lifeguards are not as unusual as you might imagine. Pigs also provide a first-class workforce. Employed for their keen sense of smell, pigs are magnificent truffle hunters.

Another misconception is that pigs are the Wayne or Waynetta Slobs of the animal kingdom.

Nothing could be further from the truth. Very well aware that cleanliness is next to godliness, they will never wee or poop anywhere through choice near their living or dining quarters. Their muddy appearance is due to the fact that they have no sweat glands (which disproves the expression 'to sweat like a pig'), and so are dependent on rolling about in mud or water to keep cool. When the mud dries it acts as sunblock and prevents them cooking to something that you'd like to shove between a couple of rounds of white-sliced with a dollop of brown sauce.

Pigs do, however, deserve their reputation as gluttons. They are omnivores and will eat anything that we eat, and quite a lot that we wouldn't, too. They gain weight quickly, piling on a pound of body weight for every three pounds of food they snort down. They have shocking table manners and if they were allowed unlimited access to the trough most hogs could tip the scales at a fat-tastic 800 lb or more!

In matters medical, pigs are more than helpful. At least forty types of medicine are made from pigs, including insulin. Pig heart valves have been used to replace human heart valves and I'm afraid pig fat is used in the production of cosmetics, wax, chalk, weedkillers and antifreeze.

Pigs are sociable beasties. They chat away with other piggies in a lingo of squeals, snorts, whistles and grunts. They like toys such as balls and old tyres and are fond of music. Not known for their own musical ability, they are loud if not tuneful: a pig squeal can reach up to 115 decibels, which is 3 decibels higher than Concorde.

There are 90 breeds and 200 varieties of pig. Their snouts are very sensitive and they have an average of 44 teeth. A sow's gestation period is 114 days. The average litter is 8–12 piglets.

You could never beat a pig in a game of Grandmother's Footsteps. Although their eyesight isn't exactly on a par with that of a hawk, pigs have a brilliant field of vision because their peepers are on the sides of their heads. So think twice before trying to creep up behind them to tweak their pigtails.

Swine Stuff

'No man should be allowed to be President who does not understand hogs.'
President Harry Truman

Boar Branch

The testosterone-fuelled playboys of the sty, a *Boar*, or *Hog*, is a male pig who has all his 'bits'.

Young, free, single and pert-teated, a *Gilt* is a lady-pig who has not yet had *Weaners*.

Suddenly in need of several Wonderbras, a *Gilt* becomes a *Sow* once she has had her first litter.

Cuter than any human sprog, *Weaners* are piglets aged 1–6 weeks.

The smallest or youngest of the litter, a *Runt* is also known, in Cornwall, as a *Piggywhidden*.

Impressively large, *Porkers* are pigs between 60–75 kg.

Scarily big, *Cutters* are pigs docking in at 76–85 kg.

The Incredible Hulks of the swine world, *Baconers* are ENORMOUS pigs that weigh from 86–104 kg.

Swine Stuff

Pigs have celebrity fans too. For instance, scrummy movie star George Clooney adores Max, his black pot-bellied pig. Lucky Max.

Great Grunters
of Literature

Pigs have appeared throughout literature in nursery rhymes, children's classics, fairy stories, poems, plays and novels. Shakespeare, Thomas Hardy, P. G. Wodehouse, Edward Lear, Walter De La Mare, Chaucer, Homer, Beatrix Potter, Ogden Nash and Roald Dahl are just a tiny handful of esteemed authors who have celebrated pink poppets in print.

Although best known as a satirical fable based on the Russian Revolution, George Orwell's classic book *Animal Farm* (1945), set in England, is more simply a cautionary tale about the exploitation of the weak and vulnerable by the strong and powerful. Telling of a revolution against tyranny that leads to a state of totalitarianism that is every bit as vile, the pigs, by self-appointment, are at the dictatorial helm. Encouraged by the pigs, the animals on Mr Jones' farm boot out their human masters and decide to run the show themselves. Initially all is hunky-dory, but then the pigs become power crazy and row between themselves. Napoleon, the porcine Stalin, does the dirty on Snowball (Trotsky) by setting the dogs on him and expelling him from the farm, thus crowning himself King of the Farmyard. From a philosophy of 'Four legs good, two legs bad', by the end of the book the pigs have come full-circle and, to the other animals, they are indistinguishable from humans. The book was originally rejected for publication but has since been established as one of the most significant books of all time.

Long before Harry Potter was so much as a flicker in J. K. Rowling's fancy, Beatrix Potter was wowing children all over the world with her long-standing nursery favourites such as Peter Rabbit, Jemima Puddleduck and Pigling Bland and his adored Pig-Wig. Potter also enthralled tots with her tale of Little Pig Robinson. Comedy actresses French and Saunders played Robinson's buxom aunts, Porcas and Dorcas, in a television adaptation of the 1990s, which gave this classic tale a modern twist. Pig-napped by a man whose favourite feast is pork crackling,

Little Pig Robinson's adventures cautioned young readers about the perils of talking to strangers.

Another favourite book that has a pig as one of the central characters is *Charlotte's Web* by E. B. White. The tale of a kind and clever little spider called Charlotte who saves Wilbur the pig from the doomed ending of most chubby piggies, the book remains as well loved today as it was when it was first published in 1952.

Swine Stuff

Big Daddy wannabes, Hereford pigs are keen wrestlers.

Hogs in History

At home…

In days gone by a 'Pigshop' sold crockery – the word 'pig' (pygge) meaning an earthenware vessel. A 'Pigman' was a seller of pots and crockery.

'Pigheaded' is the word we use to describe someone who is being stubborn. It is likely to have originated from Roman times when *caput porci* was a wedge-shaped order of attack in battle.

A 'Hog' was a shilling in Ireland and a five-shilling piece in England.

'Hogs Head' is a popular pub name as in days of yore it was a large cask of 52-gallon capacity.

Further Afield…

Model pigs, and sometimes even entire pigsties, have been discovered in ancient Chinese tombs. Pigs were regarded in China as a symbol of wealth, and it is thought that these would have been buried with the departed in order that they might take financial security with them into the next world. The dead were also interred with a supply of meat in case the next world didn't stock pork in its celestial supermarkets. The Chinese were so dotty about pigs that they included one in their zodiac calendar, though if you are born in the year of the pig you are alleged to have hedonistic tendencies and to be hopeless at making future plans.

In central Europe pigs are seen as symbols of good luck for a new year and are often depicted on cards for this festival.

The emblem of the Roman Twentieth Legion was a wild boar.

Pigs reared to be eaten used to be killed by a local 'pig killer', who simply slit the animal's throat whilst it was restrained on a 'pig bench' by stout men with ropes. Today, pig benches are much sought-after antiques, often used as furniture and no doubt gone into raptures over by smart Islington Types who proudly display them with two tons of Laura Ashley cushions.

In Ancient Greece the pig was a symbol of fertility and was a significant part of religious ceremonies and traditions.

In Ancient Egypt, where pigs were renowned for their green-trottered gardening skills, they were used to plant seeds, creating the necessary holes in the earth with their hoofs.

Swine Stuff

'This little pig went to market, this little pig stayed at home, this little pig had roast beef, and this little pig had none! This little pig cried wee, wee, wee, all the way home.'
Nursery rhyme, anon

Record-Breaking Boars

Most Expensive Pig

Selling for a phenomenal $56,000 (about £37,000), Bud, a crossbred barrow hog from Texas, USA, became the most profitable pig of all time in 1983.

Biggest Collection of Pig Paraphernalia

Representing 20 years of car-boot rooting, jumble sales and antiques hunts, Anne Langton (UK) has a collection of 9,130 pig items.

Largest Mammal to Build a Nest

The 175 kg European wild boar has such small piglets that mummy boars build nests to protect their young from predators.

Largest Litter

The largest litter recorded was the birth of 37 piglets in 1993. Incredibly, 33 survived.

Heaviest Piglet at Birth

With the average pigletty weight being 1.36 kg, pity the poor mother who in 1979 gave birth to a 2.38 kg weaner.

Biggest Pig

A record dating back to 1933, a Poland China hog called Big Bill lays claim to the title of Biggest Pig. Bill measured 5 feet from trotter to shoulder and was 9 feet long. He weighed a swoon-inducing 1,157.5 kg.

Swine Stuff

The annual World Black-Pudding Throwing Championship in Bury, Lancashire, is said to be a tradition that dates back to the Wars of the Roses.

Performing Pigs

There have been oodles of performing pigs over the years – far too many to list in a small book such as this. So, in a sort of bacon BAFTA ceremony, here's some of the greatest celebrity hams.

Perhaps the oldest performing pigs of all, *The Three Little Pigs* began life as a nursery tale. Their story has since been adapted for the stage, for various film versions and has even been nicked by Roald Dahl who rewrote it as a rhyme in which both wolf and pigs are bested by the cunning of Miss Riding Hood. The theme of the original story is simple: houses built from straw or sticks will not keep the wolf from the door. A sturdy structure of bricks and mortar – preferably with a dirty great big open fire with a vast vat of boiling water over the hearth – is the only way to keep the evil one at bay. It's also a much more sensible investment given the continually booming property market. With the wolf usually depicted with slavering jaws and evil, slitty eyes, this story is probably responsible for triggering nightmares in nurseries all over the globe.

Impossibly cute, timorous, and loyal to the end, *Piglet* is best friend to the King of the Teddies, Winnie the Pooh. Created by A. A. Milne in 1926, along with Tigger, Rabbit, Owl and Eeyore, Piglet is basically a timid kind of a chap. However, he has been known to show enormous bravery, especially when his friends have been in trouble. An evergreen children's favourite, Piglet has appeared in his very own Disney film, *Piglet's BIG Movie*.

Warner Brothers' *Porky Pig* made his screen debut in 1935 and was based on a chubby childhood chum of Director Friz Freleng. With his trademark stammer and kind heart, Porky racked up an impressive 163 cartoon appearances.

The BBC's very own *Pinky and Perky* were superstars. With a hugely successful TV show running from 1957 well into the 1970s, they performed pop songs of the day and were so beloved that they were as inundated with fan mail as the Beatles! Two Yorkshire-dwelling Czechs who had come to the UK during the Cold War, Jan and Vlasta Dalibor, created the puppet-piglet twins. Appearing alongside many celebs, including Frank Sinatra and Tom Jones, they played venues as prestigious as the London Palladium and had a regular season in Las Vegas. Even their fans were famous: the Queen Mother was reported to be very fond of the pair.

Pig, from the TV show *Pipkins*, was a loveable broad-accented Brummie. The programme itself was about a human and a group of animal puppets who ran an outfit called 'The Help

People' that did good turns. An inventor, Pig created wonderful machines, although these were usually associated in some way with food. Other characters in the show were Topov the monkey, Octavia the opera-singing ostrich and Hartley the hare. *Pipkins* ran continuously from 1973–1981, totalling 313 episodes.

All singing, all dancing and all karate-chopping, the ultimate supersty siren *Miss Piggy* shot to fame on *The Muppet Show*. Renowned for her artistic temperament, camp costumes and her adoration of Kermit the Frog (although poor Kermit often bore the brunt of her tantrums), Miss Piggy appeared with some of the greatest stars in the world – though no one was greater than the puppet diva herself. Guests who put their foot in it by making a porcine pun got extremely short shrift. Famously quoted in many collections of women's wit, her best known advice is perhaps to *'Never eat more than you can lift.'*

The Lion King's *Pumbaa* is a laid-back wild pig whose motto is *'Hakuna Matata!'* This means 'no worries for the rest of your days' in Swahili. A carouser of the first water, Pumbaa and his best mate Timon have more fun than you can shake a tusk at and live life for the moment. The cheeriest chap in the jungle, Pumbaa is loveable, cheeky, decadent… and very farty.

Babe left the world sighing a collective '*Ahh, bless!*' when the movie about the pig of the title became a bacon blockbuster. Adapting Dick King-Smith's book *The Sheep-Pig* and telling of the tiny weaner with a big heart who longed to be loved and accepted, this whimsical movie had audiences simultaneously chuckling and sniffing into their hankies. Discovering that Babe has a bit of a rapport with the sheep, Farmer Hoggett trains the small pig to round 'em up, which he does with great success simply by applying good manners and asking them nicely. Not sure that he can believe his eyes, Farmer H enters Babe for the sheepdog trials championships. Turning the onlookers' jeers into cheers, Babe and his human pal do the business and One Man and his Pig are as proud as proud can be.

A porcine Thelma and Louise, *The Tamworth Two* hit the national news headlines in 1998 when they made a break for it as they were unloaded from an abattoir lorry. Now the subjects of a BBC film, Butch and Sundance made their great escape in Malmesbury, Wiltshire. Entitled *The Legend of the Tamworth Two*, the film used real pigs – who of course hammed it up big-style.

Swine Stuff

In Korea pigs symbolise money. If you dream about pigs this is deemed to be especially fortuitous.

If Pigs Had Pop…

Some piggy songs:

Piggy Sue

Mistletoe and Swine

Pig Yellow Taxi

Walk on Sty

I Got You, Babe

Grunting High and Low

I Get Arind

Let's Sty Together

Snout!

Pig Girls Don't Cry

Piggy pop-stars:

Piggy Pop

New Pigs on the Block

Smokey-Bacon Robinson and the Miracles

Wilson Piglett

MC Ham-mer

Swine Stuff

'I like pigs. Dogs look up to us. Cats look down on us. Pigs treat us as equals.'
Sir Winston Churchill

Piggy Banks

The term 'piggy bank' originates from the Middle Ages when people kept what small sums of money they had in earthenware pots (pygges). So, nothing to do with being pink and snouty then!

Perhaps the most famous piggy banks of recent times were the National Westminster Bank pigs. Launched in 1983, a child opening an account would automatically receive *Woody*, a ceramic baby pig. When the child's savings hit the £25 mark *Annabelle*, Woody's sister, was added to the savings sty. For each additional £25 saved, another piggy bank was collected, forming a family that included *Brother Maxwell, Lady Hilary* and the super-dooper-saver pig, *Sir Nathaniel*. By

1985 one million pigs had been issued. The account was withdrawn in 1988 and no further pigs in this series were issued. The first batch of pigs were made by Sunshine ceramics, but this firm could not cope with the huge demand and Wade Ceramics later took over production.

Topping a NatWest child's achievement, perhaps, Ove Nordstrom of Sweden made it into the record books in 1957 with his 5,111 different piggy banks. To date his record is unbroken.

Swine Stuff

Because pigs eat pretty well anything they are very handy accomplices if you are planning a murder, as proven in the cult movie *Snatch* where the arch-villain feeds the remains of his victims to pigs kept for that specific purpose. If you're thinking of watching this film, be warned! *Babe* it ain't.

Oinkers in Art

Many famous artists have painted pigs. Rembrandt had a special affection for pork etchings, as did Dürer, Gainsborough, Rubens, Paul Potter, Ward and Morland. And models weren't just reproduced in paint and ink. Sculptures, carvings, masonry and ceramics, mouldings and pub signs – the pig has appeared in all sorts of art forms and all manner of poses.

The first known picture of a pig is said to have been daubed approximately forty thousand years ago and is to be found among other animal paintings on the walls of a cave in Spain.

Greek pottery dating back to the first millennium BC was often decorated with representations of pigs, and in Egypt there's a fair few depictions of sows, most of which are connected with the worship of the goddesses *Isis* and *Nut*.

In modern times pigs have often been portrayed as cheerful and amusing characters, appearing on nursery furniture and crockery and in children's picture books. They are a favourite for greetings card manufacturers and toy makers.

The world-famous glass painter, Chagall, created a picture in which a green pig featured.

Popular in Christian art, pigs pop up all over the ecclesiastical shop on choir stalls, pew ends, church masonry, embroidered wall hangings and stained glass windows. Sadly, in most cases, pigs symbolise the negative traits accorded to the poor little blighters such as gluttony and lust.

Swine Stuff

Mozart was killed by eating a pork chop. Or so says a 2001 report. Apparently, the maestro showed symptoms of a disease associated with badly cooked pork infected by a worm. However, no autopsy was carried out at the time and his death was attributed to a severe fever.

Curly Tails

Pigs Might Fly

In 1977 the hugely successful band Pink Floyd decided that they wanted a picture of a pig hovering over Battersea Power Station for their new album, *Animals*. A 40-foot zeppelin was duly transported to London, rigged up ready for launching, and an 11-strong camera crew were poised, lenses at the ready, to snap the ultimate flying pig shot. A back-up team comprising a film crew, helicopter, roadies, and a marksman (in case the porker escaped and dropped on some poor unsuspecting passer-by below) were also on standby.

The first day of the shoot was not a success. Gas cylinders blew, various problems ensued and piggy remained flightless. However, on the second day with excellent photographic conditions, it was all systems go for lift-off. The pig was raised up the side of the building and the photographers set to work. Somewhere near the top disaster struck. Or rather, a hefty gust of wind did. Snapping the mooring cable piggy did indeed fly – towards the great pigsty in the sky. Unfortunately, the marksman had not been told that he might be required again on day two and within a matter of minutes piggy had disappeared from view. But all's well that ends well: the pig was tracked down and retrieved from a farm in Kent, tidied up somewhat, and launched once more. The snappers finally got their shot.

What a Gas

A news item from Russia tells that three farmers were enjoying their lunchtime butties when they heard the squeals of a distressed pig coming from a nearby manure pit. The animal was trapped, and so one of the trio leapt in to rescue it. Overwhelmed by the pit's methane gasses our pork stuntman passed out. Rushing to his colleague's aid the second farmer threw himself into the pit, but he too collapsed. Not cottoning on to the danger below, the third man jumped into the pit also…all three men died – but the pig survived!

Albert Remembered
by my father, David Edwards

'During and just after the war my grandparents kept a pig in the unlikely setting of the spacious back garden of Ludlow Golf Club. First came George [about whom my father cannot recall his destiny] and later Albert, who was slaughtered, singed, scraped, butchered and salted within the sight of the eighteenth green. In his lifetime he had been such a favourite of my very practical gran that she went to town shopping to avoid being at the death.'

Swine Stuff

The traditional ring through a piggy's nose was a means of preventing the naughty little tinkers from digging for roots where they weren't supposed to dig for roots – like the farmer's herbaceous border.

Swine Stuff

Pigs often appear in pub names, including The Hogs Head, The Pig & Whistle and The Blue Boar. In Ludlow, Shropshire, The Blue Boar is known locally as 'The Pink Pig'. The Black Pig, a sixteenth-century Kentish inn, was built from timbers of wrecked galleons off the coast in 1558. 'Black Pig' was an English sailor's nickname for a Spanish galleon, hence the pub's name.

Perfect Pigs

To market, to market, to buy a fat pig;
Home again, home again, jiggety jig.
To market, to market, to buy a fine hog;
Home again, home again, joggety jog.
Unknown

If you're after a pig of your own then there are a few guidelines that you should observe before parting with any cash. Your checklist should include:

Piggy should be perky and look healthy and well cared for. As with dogs, his coat should be glossy.

A pig should be neither too fat nor too thin.

A good, straight belly is a must, as are straight feet. If trotters are turned out like a ballet dancer's, then don't buy!

'Buttons' (teats) should be in pairs and should average 10–16 buttons, although some breeds may have fewer.

Swine Stuff

National Pig Day is on 1 March and
November is National Pork Month.

Piggy Jokes

What do you call a crafty pig?
Cunningham

Patient: Doctor, doctor, I've got a little sty.

Doctor: Well, you had better get a
little pig then.

Why did Mrs Piggy leave Mr Piggy?
She was fed up with being taken for grunted

What do polite pigs write thank-you letters with?
Pen and Oink

A pig walks into a pub and asks for three pints of lager. He drinks and drinks and then asks the barmaid where the toilet is. She directs him to the gents and he toddles off to relieve himself.

A second pig enters the pub and asks for ten pints of lager. He drinks and drinks and then asks the barmaid where the toilet is. Once again she provides directions and he sprints down the corridor before a childish accident occurs.

Then a third pig approaches the bar and requests twenty pints of lager. The barmaid says:

'And I suppose you'll want to know where the toilet is too?'

'No,' comes the reply, 'I'm the little piggy who will be going wee, wee, wee all the way home!'

What happened when Tom stole a pig?
The pig squealed to the police

What did the little pig get from his girlfriend?
Hogs and kisses

What do you call a pig with no legs?
A groundhog

Why wouldn't the class of piglets
listen to their teacher?
Because he was an old boar

Pigs are brilliant at karate.

You don't believe me?

Well, you just watch out for their chops

*What did the piglets do for their
mum on Mother's Day?*
They threw a sowprise party

Swine Stuff

Wall Street in New York is so named because the land originally ran alongside a wall that seventeenth-century farmers built to keep their pigs from straying.

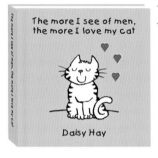

The More I See of Men,
the More I Love My Cat

Daisy Hay

Cats are better than men: fact. When was the last time you had to tell a cat not to embarrass you in public? Would a cat go out for a night on the tiles and come back smelling of anything worse than a fish supper? All the evidence is inside this book: there's nothing mad about being a catwoman!

The More I See of Men,
the More I Love my Dog

Olivia Edward

Dogs are better than men. It's obvious! They are cheaper and easier to please. They are always over the moon to see you, loyal to the last and don't care when you put on weight. And when was the last time someone engaged you in conversation by pointing at your partner and saying, 'Ahhh, that's a fine-looking beast you've got there. Can I stroke him?'

Cats: Quotes and Stuff

'Thousands of years ago, Cats were worshipped as gods. Cats have never forgotten this.'

Bursting at the seams with quotes, poems, jokes and stories, this book is a delightful celebration of the world's favourite furry friend.

The purrfect gift for every cat-lover.

Chocoheaven

Corrine Munday

This is the ultimate treat for chocolate lovers: with the history of the food of the gods to choco-myths and famous chocoholics; with choco-horoscopes, choco-games and choco-recipes. So go on, tear off the wrapper and indulge in *Chocoheaven*…

www.summersdale.com